Starting Secondary School *French*

by
Marie-Thérèse Bougard

Although every effort has been made to ensure that website addresses are correct at the time of going to press, Hodder Murray cannot be held responsible for the content of any website mentioned in this book.

Text © Marie-Thérèse Bougard 2004

First published in 2004
exclusively for WHSmith
by Hodder Murray, a member of the Hodder Headline Group
338 Euston Road
London NW1 3BH

Impression number   5 4 3 2 1
Year   2006 2005 2004

All rights reserved. Apart from any use permitted under UK copyright law, no part of this publication may be reproduced in any material form (including photocopying or storing in any medium by electronic means and whether or not transiently or incidentally to some other use of this publication) without the written permission of the Publisher, except in accordance with the provisions of the Copyright, Designs and Patents Act 1988 or under the terms of a licence issued by the Copyright Licensing Agency.

Typeset by Fakenham Photosetting Ltd, Fakenham, Norfolk
Printed and bound in Spain

A CIP catalogue record for this book is available from the British Library

ISBN 0 340 88743 5

Contents

Présentations	
Salut!	8
Au revoir!	10
Les numéros	12
Tu t'appelles comment?	14
Chez moi	
Tu habites où?	16
Ma maison	18
Ma famille	20
Mes animaux	22
J'aime	
Bon appétit!	24
Mes copains	26
Le sport	28
Récréation	30
Mes passe-temps	32

Le look	
Mes couleurs préférées	34
Le corps	36
Mes vêtements préférés	38
Petit ou grand?	40
L'école	
Mes matières préférées	42
Récréation	44
Il est quelle heure?	46
A pied ou à vélo	48
L'année	
Bon anniversaire	50
Il fait quel temps?	52
Récréation	54
Les jours de fête	56
Réponses	58

Introduction

The move from primary to secondary school can be quite an overwhelming experience. You will encounter completely new subject areas and a whole range of new topics and concepts, as well as new teachers and a new and much bigger school environment. Some people say it is like changing from being a big fish in a small pond (primary school) to being a small fish in a big pond (secondary school)!

The books in this *Starting Secondary School* series will help bridge the gap between primary and secondary school and ease the transition between the two.

 From a big fish in a small pond to a small fish in a big pond.

This introduction will answer some of the most frequently asked questions about starting secondary school.

? What are lessons like at secondary school?

You'll probably be placed in a tutor group, which meets for registration each day with the same teacher, and you are likely to stay with this group for quite a few subjects. In some subjects, like English and maths, you may be placed in a set with other children of similar ability to make it easier for everyone in the set to work at a similar pace.

The timetable is very important at secondary school. Lessons are at set times and there may be a bell signalling the end of each lesson. Different subjects are taught in different rooms and you will be told and shown where to go. It is important to get to know your timetable as quickly as possible and to know where to go for each lesson. You could fill in the blank timetable at the end of this book to help you.

? Will I be able to find my way around?

Life at secondary school may seem very different to life at primary school at first. For a start, everything seems much bigger. The buildings are bigger, the students are bigger – and there are more of them! A common fear is getting lost or not being able to find your way around. Don't worry. Your teachers will make sure you know where to go and there's always someone you can ask. Remember – if in doubt about anything, ask! Nobody will mind if you do. Everyone at the school is there to help you, and to help you to do your best.

? How do secondary schools work?

Each subject follows a scheme of work, which has been agreed by each subject department and will be based on Key Stage 3 of the National Curriculum. You will mostly study the same subjects you did at primary school. The main difference is that you will have a different teacher for each subject. You will also begin to study at least one modern foreign language, usually French or German. The choice of languages available differs from school to school.

quatre

What about tests?

It is likely that you will have more tests and assessments at secondary school than you did at primary school. You will usually be told when these are to take place and will be given plenty of time to revise and prepare for them. If you are sensible and do your homework, these tests should not worry you at all.

What about homework?

Homework is set in accordance with an agreed timetable so that you will have different subjects to deal with on different evenings. In your first year this will not be too time-consuming. A good tip is to do your homework as soon as you can, rather than leave it until the last minute and rush it. And remember to take it to school with you on the day you are supposed to hand it in!

How will I cope with the extra freedom that I will have at secondary school?

A lot of emphasis is placed on being independent and responsible in secondary school. Thinking ahead and being organised will help you a lot. Always get to your lessons on time and take everything you need with you. The teachers will tell you what you need to bring to each lesson.

How will my parents know what I am doing at school?

Most schools use a homework diary in which homework is recorded and some schools ask parents to sign this regularly to show that they have read it. It is important that your parents know what you are doing at school. This is one way of helping them find out. Don't forget to talk to them too! Your school will probably also have regular parents' evenings when your parents will be invited to school to talk to your teachers and discuss your progress.

What will French be like at secondary school?

If you have done French at primary school, you have probably concentrated on oral work, learning songs, rhymes, simple dialogues and basic phrases and vocabulary such as greetings, colours or animals. At secondary school, there will still be opportunities to sing and speak French and re-use what you already know, but you will also:

- practise speaking French with partners
- learn pronunciation skills
- listen to audio material and learn to understand spoken French
- learn to read a variety of texts in French
- learn to write accurately in French
- be expected to pay attention to details such as accents, spelling and punctuation
- study the basics of French grammar
- learn to use a bilingual dictionary
- learn about different countries where French is spoken.

cinq

How will this book help me?

This book contains many activities to help you revise basic French. It is divided into six main units:

présentations

This unit revises basic language such as yes and no, simple greetings and introductions, as well as numbers up to 12.

chez moi

This unit revises language used to talk about different countries, your home, your family and pets.

j'aime

This unit revises language used to talk about food and drink, friends and hobbies, as well as numbers up to 30.

le look

This unit revises language used to talk about colours, the body, clothes and simple descriptions of people.

l'école

This unit revises the names of school subjects, days of the week and the time, as well as numbers up to 69.

l'année

This unit revises the names of the months and seasons, phrases to do with the weather, birthdays and holidays, as well as numbers up to 100.

What's in each unit?

Each of the six units is made up of four or five self-contained spreads. Each spread has activities for you to do: simple cartoons to read, crosswords, wordsearches, quizzes, games and puzzles.

Each spread has two sections to help you with the language:

'Dico' is slang for 'dictionnaire', the French word for 'dictionary'. This section lists all the new words and expressions used on that spread.

bons points

'Bons points' can mean either 'good points' or 'good marks'. With arrows pointing at various words and phrases, this section provides helpful hints for good pronunciation as well as simple grammar explanations.

The following section appears on most spreads:

par cœur

'Par cœur' means 'by heart' and it is recommended you learn its contents by heart.
In most cases it includes made-up rhymes to help you remember useful vocabulary and concentrate on good pronunciation.
Some of these sections refer to **moi... moi... moi...**, and you are encouraged to write simple sentences about yourself and learn them by heart. It will help build your confidence so you can have simple conversations in French about things that matter to you.

Most units include at least one of the following sections:

mots croisés

This is French for 'crossword', and these grids will help you revise key vocabulary.

moi... moi... moi...

'Moi' means 'me'. This section is for you to illustrate with your own drawings or photographs, and fill in with details about your own life.

pour jouer

'Jouer' means 'to play'. This section includes simple board games for you to play with a friend. You will need dice and counters for these.

pour chanter

'Chanter' means 'to sing'. There are three songs included in this book. The lyrics of the first two were specially written for you to revise and remember key language. The third one is a popular Christmas song that uses a lot of words you will already be familiar with. All three songs are to traditional tunes, and the music scores have been included – you may find them useful if you play the piano, keyboard, flute or recorder.

You will also find two sections called **sondage**.

'Sondage' means 'opinion poll'. These sections use basic vocabulary, such as colours or qualities, as a starting point. You will be asked to state your own preferences and ask a friend or two to do the same, and then compare the results.

Enjoy your workbook!
Amuse-toi bien!

présentations

bons points

- Pronounce '**salut**' as if there were no 't' at the end.

- Say your 'r's from the back of the throat.

- '**Ça va**' can be used either as a question meaning 'How are you?' or as a reply meaning 'I'm fine'.

huit

1 salut!

Read the cartoon story, and find the French for:
1. hi — Salut
2. yes — oui
3. no — non
4. help — Au secours
5. thank you — merci
6. are you OK? — ça va
7. I'm OK — ça va
8. and you? — et toi

Choose the right label for each bubble.

au secours! 4   merci 2

salut! 1   ça va? 3

mini-dico

au secours!	help!
ça va	I'm fine/OK
ça va?	how are you?/ are you OK?
et toi?	and you?
merci	thank you
non	no
oui	yes
salut	hi

par cœur

Learn this by heart.

Salut, Lulu!
Ça va, Sarah?
Merci, Henri.

neuf

présentations

bons points

- Do not pronounce the final 'd' of 'Edouard'.

- 'Bonsoir', 'au revoir', 'Omar' and 'Edouard' rhyme: they all end with the same 'ar' sound.

- Do not pronounce the 't' of 'nuit'. 'Nuit' rhymes with 'Annie'.

2 au revoir!

Look at the cartoons, and find the French for:
1. goodbye — *Au revoir*
2. good evening — *bonsoir*
3. good morning — *bonjour*
4. good night — *Bonne nuit*
5. please — *s'il te plaît*

dix

Insert all the missing vowels.

mini-dico

au revoir	goodbye
bonjour	good morning, hello
bonne nuit	good night
bonsoir	good evening
s'il te plaît	please

par cœur

Learn this by heart.

Bonsoir, Omar!
Au revoir, Edouard!
Bonne nuit, Annie!

onze

présentations

bons points

- Say '**deux**' as if there were no 'x' at the end.

- Say '**trois**' as if there were no 's' at the end.

- '**Six**' and '**dix**' both sound as if the 'x' were a double 's'.

douze

3 les numéros

mots croisés

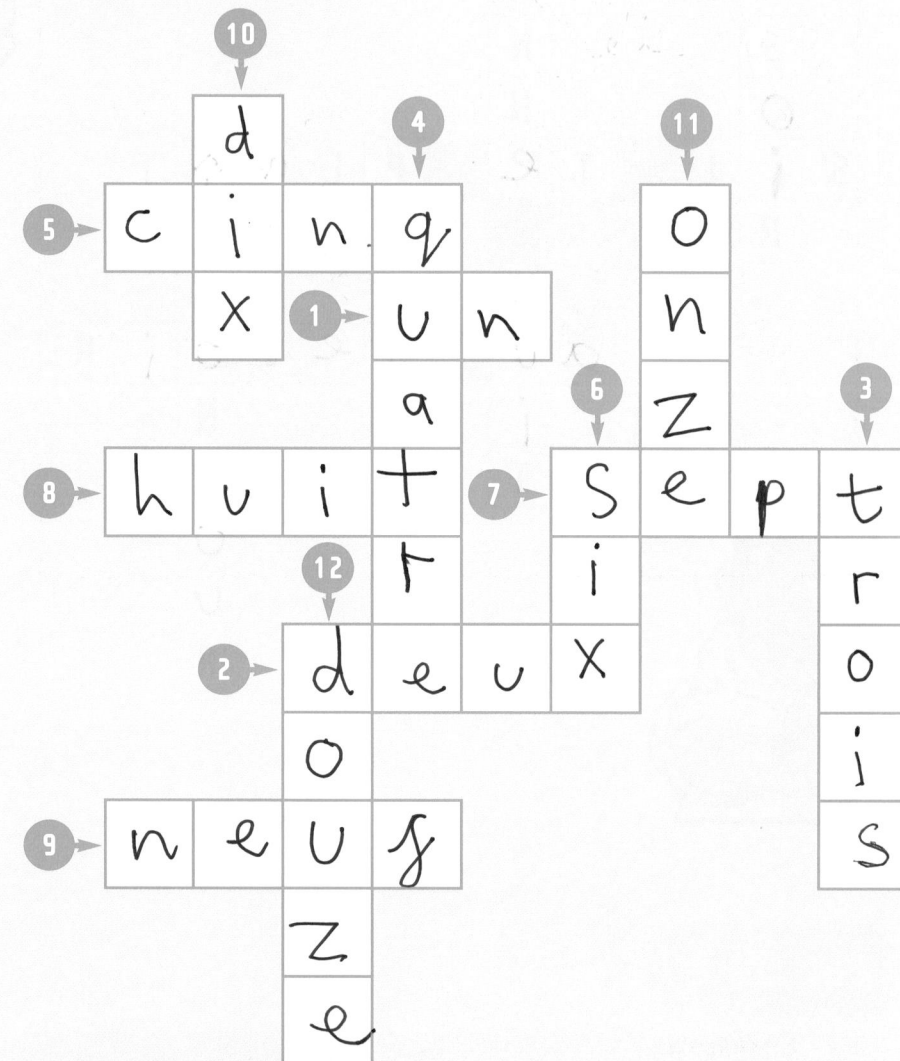

Which number rhymes with which name?

2 – deux	Alice
3 – trois	Annette
6 – six	François
7 – sept	Madame Ventouse
9 – neuf	Matthieu
12 – douze	Monsieur Lebœuf

Join the dots to find out what Milou is doing.

mini-dico

un	1
deux	2
trois	3
quatre	4
cinq	5
six	6
sept	7
huit	8
neuf	9
dix	10
onze	11
douze	12

par cœur

Learn this by heart.

1, 2, 3, François!
4, 5, 6, Alice!
7, 8, 9, Monsieur Lebœuf!
10, 11, 12, Madame Ventouse!

treize

présentations

bons points

- 'Tu as quel âge?', the French way of saying 'How old are you?' means – literally – 'What age do you have?'

- That is the reason why the answer starts with 'J'ai...' which means 'I have'.

J'ai onze ans

4 tu t'appelles comment?

Read the cartoon story, and find the French for:
1. How old are you? .....Tu as quel âge?.....
2. What's your name? .....Tu t'appelles?.....
3. My name is... .....Je m'appelle......

It's the first day at a new school. Alex, Julie and Sam are nervous – they don't know anybody...

Who is the youngest? Alex, Julie or Sam? .....Alex.....
Who is the oldest? Alex, Julie or Sam? .....Sam.....

quatorze

moi... moi... moi...

Stick a picture of yourself (or draw one) in the space and complete the speech bubble with information about your name and your age.

Bonjour! Je m'appelle ....Leah....
J'ai ....10 dix........ ans.

by heart.
par cœur

When you have completed the speech bubble, learn it by heart.

mini-dico

j'ai ... ans
I'm ... years old

je m'appelle ...
my name's ...

Tu as quel âge?
How old are you?

Tu t'appelles comment?
What's your name?

quinze

chez moi

bons points

- When saying where you live, introduce the town or city with 'à'.

- Most names of countries are introduced with 'en', but there are exceptions: 'le Canada' and 'le pays de Galles' are introduced with 'au'.
'les USA' is introduced with 'aux'.

5 tu habites où?

Look at the speech bubbles and match each town with the correct country.

Aberystwyth ... est aux USA.
Birmingham ... est en Suisse.
Bruxelles ... est en Ecosse.
Glasgow ... est en France.
Chicago ... est en Irlande.
Québec ... est au Canada.
Genève ... est en Belgique.
Dublin ... est en Angleterre.
Paris ... est au pays de Galles.

mots croisés

Horizontalement ▶
- 2 New York est aux USA
- 3 Glasgow est en ecosse
- 6 Dublin est en Irlande
- 9 Manchester est en angleterre
- 10 Québec est au canada

Verticalement ▼
- 1 Aberystwyth est au pays de galles
- 4 Genève est en suisse
- 5 Bruxelles est en belgique
- 7 Cardiff est au gall de Galles ✱
- 8 Calais est en suisse ✱

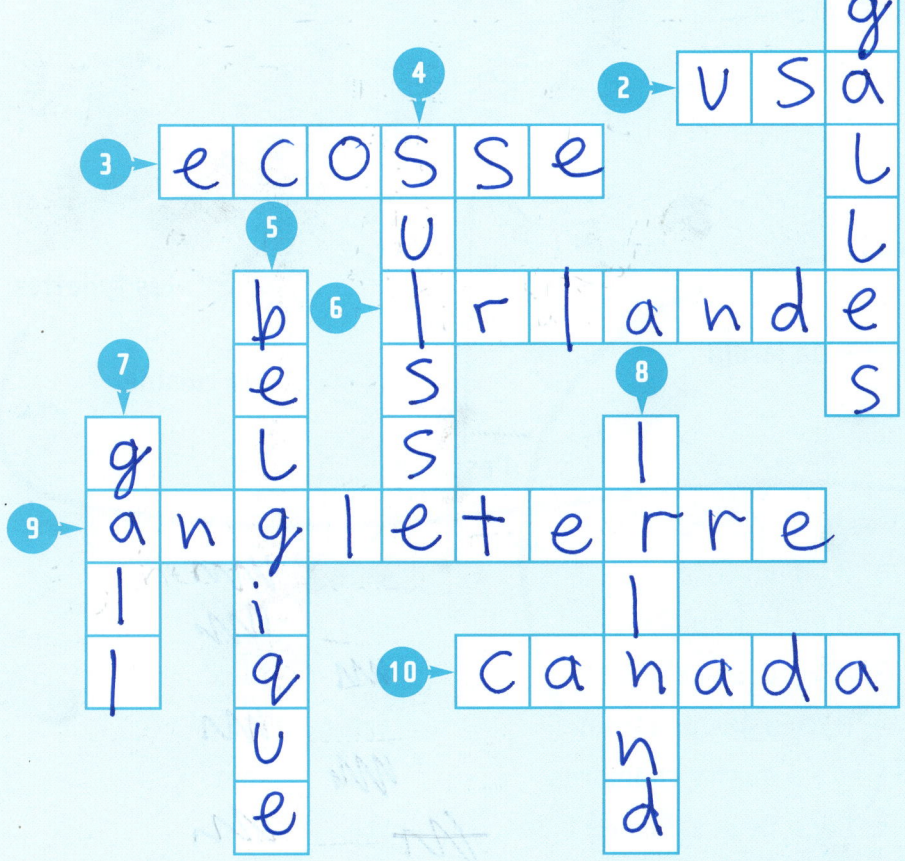

mini-dico

l'Angleterre	England
la Belgique	Belgium
le Canada	Canada
l'Écosse	Scotland
la France	France
l'Irlande	Ireland
le pays de Galles	Wales
la Suisse	Switzerland
les USA	the USA
à	in
au(x)	in
en	in
est	is
j'habite	I live
tu habites où?	where do you live?

par cœur

Learn this by heart.

Tu habites où?
1, 2, 3, au Canada?
4, 5, 6, en Suisse?
7, 8, 9, à Châteauneuf?
10, 11, 12,
j'habite à Toulouse.

dix-sept

chez moi

bons points

- 'Il y a' means both 'there is' and 'there are'.

- When talking about what's missing, use 'de' after 'il n'y a pas'.

- 'Salle de bains' rhymes with 'jardin'. Do not pronounce the 's' at the end of 'bains'.

- 'Toilettes' sounds quite different from 'toilet'. The first syllable sounds the same as 'toi' in 'et toi?' (see page 9). Do not pronounce the 's' at the end of the word.

6 ma maison

Look at the picture for three minutes, then hide it and do the memory quiz below.

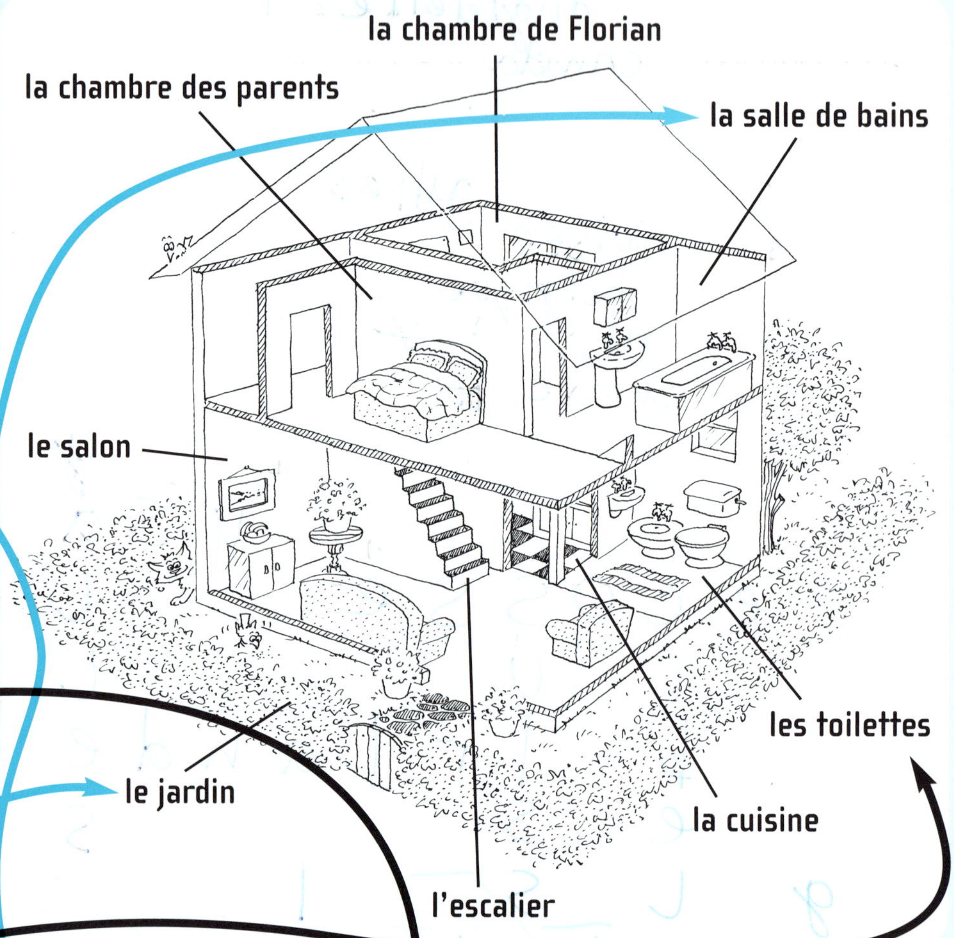

la chambre de Florian
la chambre des parents
la salle de bains
le salon
les toilettes
le jardin
la cuisine
l'escalier

1 Il y a un escalier.   vrai
2 Il y a une cuisine.   vrai
3 Il y a deux salons.   faux
4 Il n'y a pas de jardin.   vrai
5 Il y a quatre chambres.   faux
6 Il y a deux salles de bains. vrai

dix-huit

Find in the grid the French for:
1 bedroom — chambre
2 garden — jardin
3 house — maison
4 kitchen — cuisine
5 sitting room — salon
6 staircase — escalier
7 toilet — toilettes

```
•  E  S  C  A  L  I  E  R
T  O  I  L  E  T  T  E  S
S  S  C  U  I  S  I  N  E
A  A  L  L  E  D  E  B  A
L  I  J  A  R  D  I  N  N
O  C  H  A  M  B  R  E  S
N  M  A  I  S  O  N  •  •
```

The remaining letters make up the name of another room. What is it?
....

mini-dico

la chambre	bedroom
la cuisine	kitchen
l'escalier	staircase
le jardin	garden
la salle de bains	bathroom
le salon	sitting room
les toilettes	toilet
faux	false
vrai	true
il y a …	there is/are …
il n'y a pas de …	there is no …

par cœur

Learn this by heart.

A la maison,
Louison est dans le salon,
Karine est dans la cuisine.
Antoinette est aux toilettes
et Justin est dans le jardin.

chez moi

bons points

- To say 'Fabien's brother' or 'Fabien's sister' in French, you need to say 'the brother of Fabien' or 'the sister of Fabien'. The French for 'of' is '**de**'.

- The French for 'my' is '**mon**' when it is followed by a masculine word.

- The French for 'my' is '**ma**' when it is followed by a feminine word.

- The French for 'my' is '**mes**' when it is followed by a word in the plural.

vingt

7 ma famille

Look at the pictures of Fabien's family, and find the French for:

1 brother — frère
2 sister — soeur
3 father — père
4 mother — mère
5 grandfather — grand-père
6 grandmother — grand-mère
7 stepfather — beau-père
8 stepmother — beau-mère
9 stepsister — demi-soeur

La famille de Fabien

Which picture fits the description? ....tois....

*Voici ma famille: mes grands-parents,
ma mère et mon beau-père,
mon frère (Pierre), ma demi-sœur (Océane)
et... moi (Thomas)!*

pour jouer

Use the family grid on page 20 to play with one or two friends.

You need one die and three counters, and a piece of paper and pen for each player.

Each player chooses three characters from the grid and writes their names on their sheet of paper. Player 1 places a counter on a blank box of their choice, casts the die and moves the counter accordingly. If the counter lands on a box with one of the characters he/she had chosen, Player 1 continues with the second counter. If not, it is the next player's turn.

You can move the counters:
from left to right ▶
from right to left ◀
from top to bottom ▼
from bottom to top ▲
But you cannot move diagonally.

The winner is the first person with all three counters on the correct boxes.

mini-dico

le beau-père	stepfather
la belle-mère	stepmother
la demi-sœur	stepsister
le frère	brother
la grand-mère	grandmother
le grand-père	grandfather
les grands-parents	grandparents
la mère	mother
le père	father
la sœur	sister
de	of
ma	my
mes	my
mon	my
voici	here's

vingt et un

chez moi

bons points

- You need to pronounce 'un ours' as if 'ours' started with an 'n'. You need to pronounce the 's' at the end.

- You need to pronounce 'un éléphant' as if 'éléphant' started with an 'n'. Do not pronounce the 't' at the end.

8 mes animaux

Which animals can you see in Diane's bedroom?

Dans la chambre de Diane, il y a …

1. un chat — oui — ~~non~~
2. un ours — ~~oui~~ — non
3. un lapin — oui — ~~non~~
4. un chien — ~~oui~~ — non
5. un cheval — oui — ~~non~~
6. une girafe — oui — ~~non~~
7. un serpent — oui — ~~non~~
8. un poisson — oui — ~~non~~
9. un hamster — ~~oui~~ — non
10. un éléphant — oui — ~~non~~

vingt-deux

moi... moi... moi...

Stick down a picture of your family and/or your pets, and complete the speech bubble.

J'ai *moi famie + 2 chat*.
Je n'ai pas de *fame + chat*.

mini-dico

un chat	cat
un cheval	horse
un chien	dog
un éléphant	elephant
une girafe	giraffe
un hamster	hamster
un lapin	rabbit
un ours	bear
un poisson	fish
un serpent	snake

par cœur

When you have completed the speech bubble, learn it by heart.

vingt-trois 23

bons points

- 'Tu as faim?' means literally 'do you have hunger?'

- 'Tu as soif?' means literally 'do you have thirst?'

9 bon appétit!

Find the right illustration for each item on the menu.

Tu as faim?
- sandwich au fromage
- sandwich au jambon
- sandwich au poulet
- frites
- salade
- pizza aux champignons
- glace à la vanille
- glace à la fraise
- gâteau au chocolat

Tu as soif?
- eau minérale
- jus d'orange
- limonade

Choose what you would like from the menu and complete the speech bubbles.

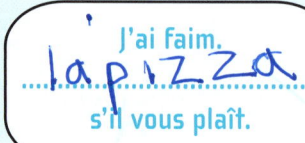

J'ai faim. la pizza s'il vous plaît.

J'ai soif. Jambon s'il vous plaît.

mots croisés

Horizontalement ▶
1. un jus d'orange, s'il vous plaît
4. un _____ au fromage ou au poulet?
6. j'ai ____: un sandwich, s'il vous plaît
9.
10. une ___ minérale, s'il vous plaît
11.

Verticalement ▼
2. j'ai ____: une eau minérale, s'il vous plaît
3. une glace à la fraise ou à la _____?
5.
7. un sandwich au jambon ou au _____?
8. une _____ à la vanille ou à la fraise?

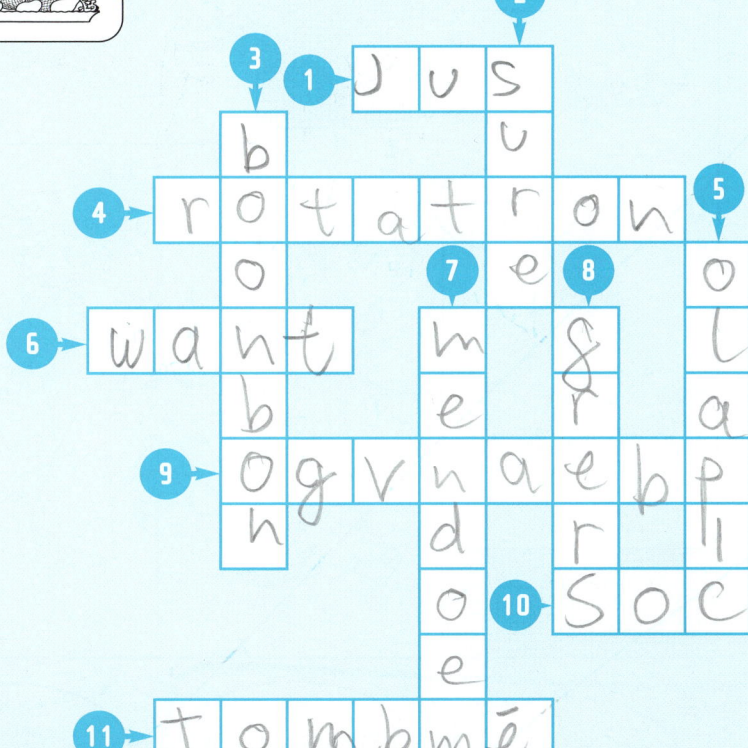

mini-dico

le champignon	mushroom
le chocolat	chocolate
l'eau minérale	mineral water
la fraise	strawberry
les frites	chips
le fromage	cheese
le gâteau	cake
la glace	ice cream
le jambon	ham
le jus d'orange	orange juice
la limonade	lemonade
la pizza	pizza
le poulet	chicken
la salade	salad
le sandwich	sandwich
la vanille	vanilla
j'ai faim	I'm hungry
j'ai soif	I'm thirsty
tu as faim?	are you hungry?
tu as soif?	are you thirsty?
bon appétit	enjoy your meal
s'il vous plaît	please

par cœur

When you have completed the speech bubbles on page 24, learn them by heart.

vingt-cinq

bons points

- Most French adjectives change depending on whether the word they are describing is masculine or feminine.

- Most feminine adjectives need an extra 'e' at the end.

- The feminine of '**généreux**' is '**généreuse**'.

- The feminine of '**sportif**' is '**sportive**'.

- '**Sympa**' remains the same whether it is masculine or feminine.

vingt-six

10 mes copains

Read the bubbles to find out each person's name and write them down.

Blablabla et patati ...

Ma copine s'appelle Julie. Elle est sympa.

Mon copain s'appelle Luc. Il est marrant.

Ma copine s'appelle Karima. Elle est bavarde.

Ma copine s'appelle Océane. Elle est sportive.

Mon copain s'appelle Hamid. Il est intelligent.

Mon copain s'appelle Matthieu. Il est généreux.

sondage

What's most important in a friend?
Number these qualities in order of importance to you,
then ask two friends and see if you agree.
(1 = most important; 7 = least important)

Le hit-parade des qualités			
	moi	1	2
cool			
calme			
sympa			
sportif/sportive			
marrant/marrante			
généreux/généreuse			
intelligent/intelligente			

mini-dico

mon copain	my (boy)friend
ma copine	my (girl)friend
bavard/bavarde	chatty
généreux/généreuse	generous
intelligent/intelligente	clever
marrant/marrante	funny
sportif/sportive	sporty
sympa	nice, friendly
s'appelle	is called
il est	he is
elle est	she is

par cœur

Learn this by heart.

Raoul est cool,
Malika est sympa,
Matthieu est généreux
Et Florian est marrant!

vingt-sept

bons points

- Pronounce '**natation**' and '**équitation**' as if they ended in 'ssion', and make them rhyme with 'non'.

- Do not say the 't' at the end of '**sport**'. Pronounce the 'r' from the back of your throat.

vingt-huit

11 le sport

Do this quiz and find out how sporty you are.

Tu aimes le football (ou le basket)?	Tu aimes le judo (ou le karaté)?	Tu aimes le ski (ou la luge)?
NON ↓	NON ↓	OUI →
Tu aimes la natation?	Tu aimes l'équitation?	Tu aimes la marche à pied?
NON ↓	NON ↓	OUI →
Tu aimes courir?	Tu aimes le vélo?	Tu aimes la voile (ou la planche à voile)?
NON ↓	NON ↓	OUI →
Aïe! Tu n'es pas très sportif/sportive ...	Pas mal!	Tu es très sportif/sportive! Super!

Complete the bubbles.

par cœur

Learn this by heart.

Le sport, d'accord!
La marche à pied et le karaté, OK!
La voile, génial!
Mais le ski, non merci!
L'équitation, attention!
Et la natation, non, non, non!

mini-dico

le basket	basketball
courir	to run
l'équitation	horseriding
le football	football
le judo	judo
le karaté	karate
la luge	sledging
la marche à pied	walking
la natation	swimming
la planche à voile	windsurfing
le ski	skiing
le vélo	cycling
la voile	sailing
aïe!	ouch!
d'accord	OK
génial/e	brilliant
pas mal	not bad
super	great
très	very

vingt-neuf

bons points

- Say 'quatorze' and 'quinze' as if they started with a 'k'. Don't pronounce the 'u'.

- Don't pronounce the 't' in 'vingt' except in 'vingt-deux', 'vingt-trois' etc.

12 récréation

How many numbers can you see in the grid?

```
T  R  E  I  Z  E  Q
Q  R  D  V  I  N  U
U  G  E  E  T  Q  A
I  U  N  N  U  U  T
N  A  T  R  T  X  O
Z  S  E  I  Z  E  R
E  V  I  N  G  T  Z
E  D  O  U  Z  E  E
```

The remaining letters make up another number. What is it?
....

Complete the series.

1 treize, seize, dix-neuf, vingt-deux, ...
2 vingt-huit, vingt-six, vingt-quatre, ...
3 dix, quinze, vingt, vingt-cinq, ...
4 dix-neuf, dix-sept, quinze, ...
5 quatorze, seize, dix-huit, ...
6 onze, quinze, ...

trente

pour chanter

You can sing this to the tune of 'Au clair de la lune'.

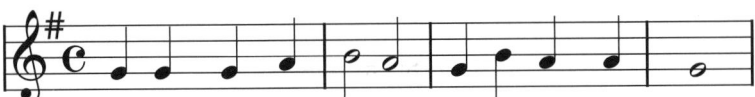
Je m'ap-pelle Ca- mi-lle, j'ha-bite à Mou-lins
Ma co- pine Pau-li-ne a- dore les pi- zzas.

A- vec ma fa- mi-lle: une sœur et trois chiens.
Elle aime la va- ni- lle et le cho-co- lat.

Ma sœur s'ap-pelle Li- ne, je n'ai pas de frère,
Elle est très spor-ti- ve, elle fait du ju- do

mais dans la cui- si- ne, il y a mon ham-ster.
a- vec A- man- di-ne et a- vec Thé- o.

Je m'appelle Camille
J'habite à Moulins
Avec ma famille
Une sœur et trois chiens.

Ma sœur s'appelle Line
Je n'ai pas de frère
Mais dans la cuisine
Il y a mon hamster.

Ma copine Pauline
Adore les pizzas.
Elle aime la vanille
Et le chocolat.

Elle est très sportive
Elle fait du judo
Avec Amandine
Et avec Théo.

mini-dico

treize	13
quatorze	14
quinze	15
seize	16
dix-sept	17
dix-huit	18
dix-neuf	19
vingt	20
vingt et un	21
vingt-deux	22
vingt-trois	23
vingt-quatre	24
vingt-cinq	25
vingt-six	26
vingt-sept	27
vingt-huit	28
vingt-neuf	29
trente	30

trente et un

bons points

- Here is a list of other hobbies to help you:

peindre – to paint
dessiner – to draw
faire du théâtre – to do drama
faire la cuisine – to cook
regarder la télé – to watch TV
jouer du piano – to play the piano
aller au cinéma – to go to the cinema
écouter de la musique – to listen to music

trente-deux

13 mes passe-temps

Read the cartoon story and find the French for:
1 playing cards ....
2 computers ....
3 reading ....
4 dancing ....
5 I like that ....
6 I hate that ....

moi... moi... moi...

Stick in a picture illustrating your favourite hobbies.
Then complete the speech bubble
saying what you like doing in your spare time.

mini-dico

> J'aime
> fair de ski
> et danser.

la flûte	flute
l'ordinateur	computer
le passe-temps	hobby
j'aime ça	I like that
je déteste ça	I hate that
danser	to dance
jouer aux cartes	to play cards
jouer de la flûte	to play the flute
lire	to read

par cœur

When you have completed the speech bubble,
learn it by heart.

trente-trois

le look

bons points

- 'Marron' doesn't mean 'maroon', it means 'brown'.

- The French for 'maroon' is 'bordeaux'.

14 mes couleurs préférées

Colour in each box according to the captions.

les trois couleurs primaires:

| rouge | jaune | bleu |

les couleurs complémentaires:

| rouge | et | vert |

| jaune | et | violet |

| bleu | et | orange |

trente-quatre

sondage

Number each colour in order of preference, then ask two friends and see if you have similar tastes.
(1 = favourite; 12 = least favourite)

le hit-parade des couleurs			
	moi	1	2
bleu			
rouge			
jaune			
orange			
vert			
violet			
noir			
gris			
blanc			
rose			
bordeaux			
marron			

par cœur

Draw a rainbow and learn this by heart.

Violet, indigo, bleu,
Vert, jaune,
Orange, rouge
C'est l'arc-en-ciel!

mini-dico

l'arc-en-ciel	rainbow
la couleur	colour
préféré	favourite
blanc	white
bleu	blue
bordeaux	maroon
gris	grey
indigo	indigo
jaune	yellow
marron	brown
noir	black
orange	orange
rose	pink
rouge	red
vert	green
violet	purple

trente-cinq

le look

bons points

- The French for 'hair' is always plural. Do not pronounce the 'x' at the end.

- Pronounce 'les yeux' as if 'yeux' started with a 'z'. Do not pronounce the 'x' at the end.

15 le corps

Roméo le robot

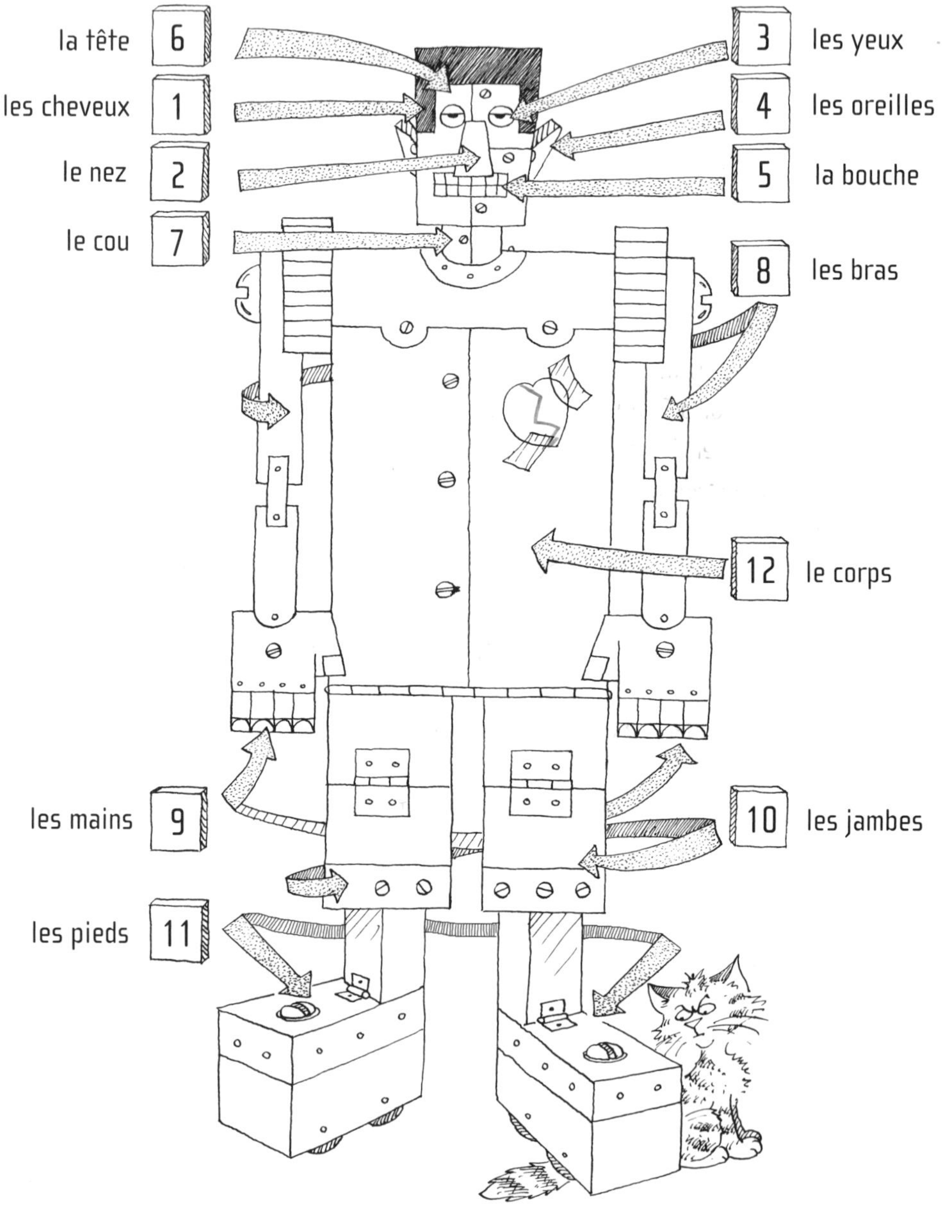

la tête 6	3 les yeux
les cheveux 1	4 les oreilles
le nez 2	5 la bouche
le cou 7	8 les bras
	12 le corps
les mains 9	10 les jambes
les pieds 11	

trente-six

Look at Roméo le robot, and find the French for:
1 eyes ....
2 feet ....
3 hair ....
4 arms ....
5 nose ....
6 head ....
7 body ....
8 mouth ....

pour jouer

Use the picture on page 36 to play with one or two friends.

- You need two dice, and a piece of paper and pen for each player.
- Players take it in turn to throw one or two dice. To start, you need to throw a 12 or a 6. If you throw a 6, you can draw the head on your piece of paper. If you throw a 12, you can draw the body. Then you continue, drawing another part of the robot according to what number you have thrown.
- You cannot draw the hair, eyes, ears, nose or mouth if you haven't drawn the head.
- You cannot draw the arms, hands, legs and feet until you have drawn the body.
- You cannot draw the neck until you have drawn either the body or the head.
- The first player with a complete robot wins the game.

mini-dico

la bouche	mouth
le bras	arm
les cheveux	hair
le corps	body
le cou	neck
la jambe	leg
la main	hand
le nez	nose
l'oreille	ear
le pied	foot
la tête	head
les yeux	eyes

trente-sept

le look

bons points

- In French, 'le pantalon' and 'le jean' are singular – unless you are talking about more than one pair. In the same way, the French for 'pyjamas' is 'le pyjama'.

- The 'eau' of 'manteau' and 'chapeau' is pronounced as 'o'.

16 mes vêtements préférés

Look at the clothes and add colours and patterns to suit your own taste and style.

le tee-shirt	la chemise	le sweat	le pull
le pantalon	la robe	le jean	la jupe
le manteau	le blouson	la veste	le chapeau
les chaussettes	les chaussures	les baskets	les bottes
la cravate	l'écharpe	le collant	les gants

Find the French for:

1 trousers ....   3 shoes ....

2 jacket ....   4 tie ....

trente-huit

Follow the description below to complete the picture of the prime suspect.

Le suspect porte un manteau bleu, un jean gris et des bottes marron. Il porte un chapeau rouge, une écharpe verte et des gants noirs.

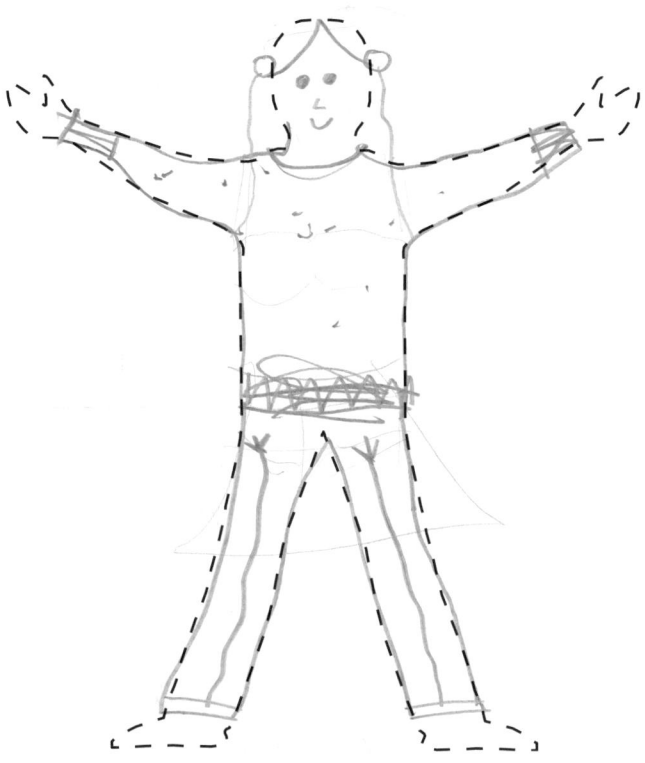

mini-dico

les baskets	trainers
le blouson	bomber jacket
les bottes	high boots
le chapeau	hat
les chaussettes	socks
les chaussures	shoes
la chemise	shirt
le collant	tights
la cravate	tie
l'écharpe	scarf
les gants	gloves
le jean	jeans
la jupe	skirt
le manteau	coat
le pantalon	trousers
le pull	sweater
la robe	dress
le sweat	sweatshirt
le tee-shirt	t-shirt
la veste	jacket
les vêtements	clothes
porte	is wearing

par cœur

Learn this by heart.

J'aime la veste verte d'Yvette,
les gants blancs de Bertrand
et la cravate d'Agathe,
mais je déteste les chaussettes violettes de Josette!

trente-neuf

le look

bons points

- When describing a girl, you need to use the feminine form of adjectives, and say 'elle est petite' or 'elle est grande'.

- The feminine form of 'gros' is 'grosse'.

- If you wear glasses, say 'je porte des lunettes'.

- If you are neither tall nor small, say 'je suis de taille moyenne'.

quarante

17 petit ou grand?

Read the cartoon story, and find the French for:
1 long hair ....
2 blue eyes ....
3 brown eyes ....
4 slim ....
5 tall ....
6 small ....

Là, j'ai huit ans...

... je suis petit et gros!

Là... tu es grand et mince. Tu as les cheveux longs!

Oui, j'ai les cheveux longs... et bruns!

Ah, une photo de ma maman, mais... elle a les yeux bleus! Maman a les yeux marron.

Mmm... Ce n'est pas ta maman. C'est ta grand-mère...

moi... moi... moi...

Stick in a picture of yourself and complete the description.

Je suis..............................

par cœur

When you have completed the description, learn it by heart.

mini-dico

grand/grande	tall
petit/petite	small
gros/grosse	fat
mince	slim
long/longue	long
court/courte	short
elle a	she has
j'ai	I have
je suis	I am
tu as	you have
tu es	you are
c'est	it is
ce n'est pas	it is not
là	there

quarante et un

l'école

bons points

- The 'que' of 'musique' and 'informatique' is pronounced as 'k'.

- Pronounce the 'r's in 'mardi', 'mercredi' and 'vendredi' from the back of the throat.

- 'Sciences' rhymes with 'Clémence' – do not pronounce the 's' at the end.

- 'Sport' rhymes with 'Nestor' – do not pronounce the 't' at the end.

quarante-deux

18 mes matières préférées

Put back all the missing vowels.

```
            J   D
    M   R C R   D
            M       S
                D
    R           D
L N D           N   M
                C
                H   D
        V N D R     D
```

Find the right symbol for each school subject.

sport   français   musique
maths   histoire   géographie
anglais   sciences   informatique

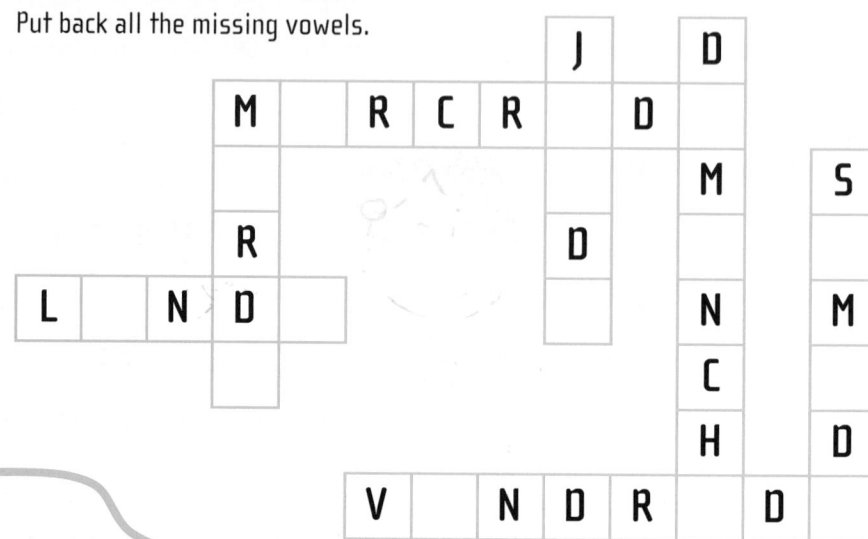

Read the bubbles and look at the timetable.
Is it Julien's or Samia's?

J'aime le mardi, parce que j'ai sport et musique. La prof de sport est très sympa et j'adore la musique: c'est ma matière préférée.

Je déteste le jeudi. J'ai anglais et géographie. Je déteste la géographie et je n'aime pas le prof d'anglais.

mini-dico

	lundi	mardi	mercredi	jeudi	vendredi	samedi
8h–9h	français	maths		sciences		informatique
9h–10h	maths	maths		géographie	maths	anglais
			récréation			
10h15–11h15	dessin	français		français	anglais	sport
11h15–12h15	histoire	anglais		musique	informatique	sport
			déjeuner			
13h45–14h45	sciences	dessin		anglais	français	
14h45–15h45	sport	sciences		histoire / géo	français	
			récréation			
16h–17h	sport			français		

par cœur

Learn this by heart.

Sophie déteste la géographie,
Clémence aime les sciences,
Grégoire aime l'histoire,
et Nestor adore le sport!

l'école, le collège	school
l'anglais	English
le dessin	art
le français	French
la géographie	geography
l'histoire	history
l'informatique	ICT
les maths	maths
la matière	school subject
la musique	music
les sciences	science
le sport	PE
lundi	Monday
mardi	Tuesday
mercredi	Wednesday
jeudi	Thursday
vendredi	Friday
samedi	Saturday
dimanche	Sunday

quarante-trois

bons points

- Say '**soixante**' as if the 'x' were a double 's'.

- Say '**quarante**' and '**cinquante**' as if the 'qu' were a 'k'.

quarante-quatre

19 récréation

Follow the numbers in the maze in order to go from the entrance to the exit safely.

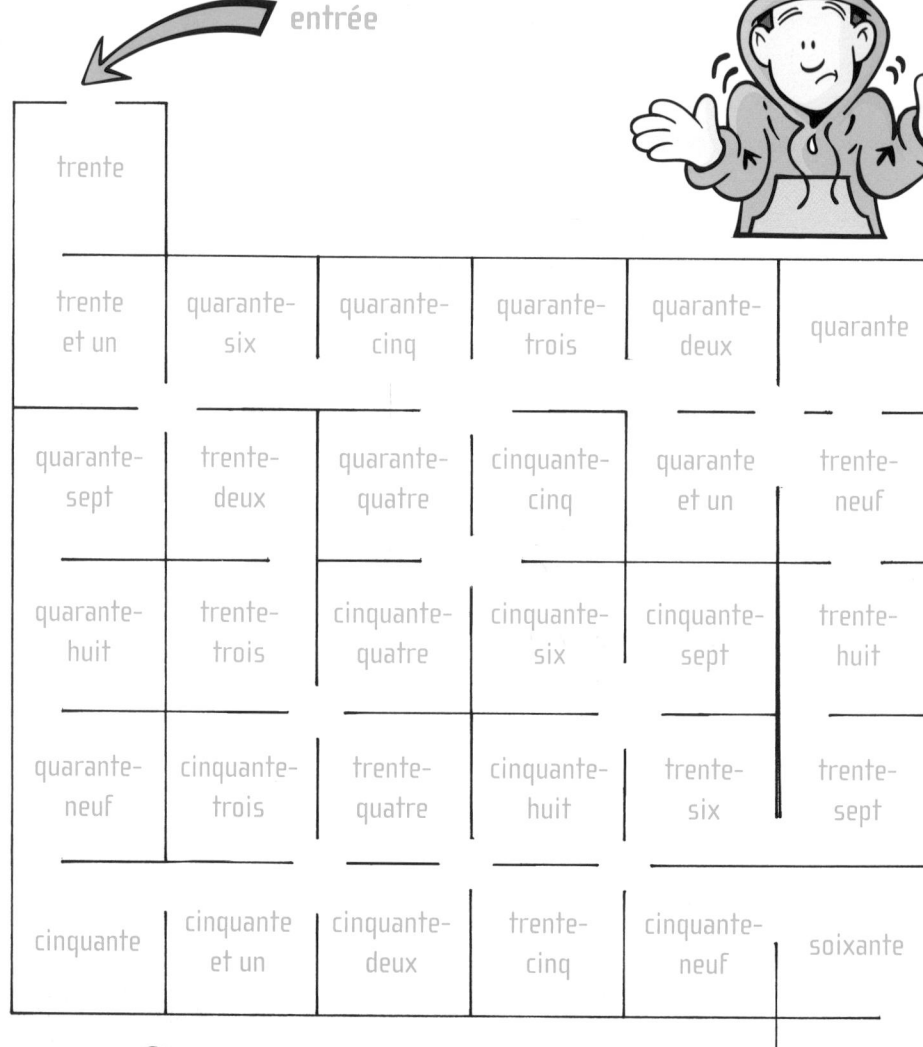

entrée

trente					
trente et un	quarante-six	quarante-cinq	quarante-trois	quarante-deux	quarante
quarante-sept	trente-deux	quarante-quatre	cinquante-cinq	quarante et un	trente-neuf
quarante-huit	trente-trois	cinquante-quatre	cinquante-six	cinquante-sept	trente-huit
quarante-neuf	cinquante-trois	trente-quatre	cinquante-huit	trente-six	trente-sept
cinquante	cinquante et un	cinquante-deux	trente-cinq	cinquante-neuf	soixante
					soixante et un

sortie

pour chanter

You can sing this to the tune of 'Frère Jacques'.

Lun- di ma- tin
Mar- di ma- tin
Jeu- di ma- tin

J'ai his- toire
J'ai mu- sique
J'ai fran- çais

J'aime l'é-cole, j'aime l'his-toire
J'aime le prof de mu- sique
Ma ma-tière pré- fé- rée

C'est su- per!
Il est sym- pa!
C'est gé- nial!

Lundi matin,
Lundi matin,
J'ai histoire,
J'ai histoire.
J'aime l'école, j'aime l'histoire,
J'aime l'école, j'aime l'histoire.
C'est super!
C'est super!

Mardi matin,
Mardi matin,
J'ai musique,
J'ai musique.
J'aime le prof de musique,
J'aime le prof de musique.
Il est sympa!
Il est sympa!

Jeudi matin,
Jeudi matin,
J'ai français,
J'ai français,
Ma matière préférée,
Ma matière préférée.
C'est génial!
C'est génial!

mini-dico

trente et un	31
trente-deux	32
trente-trois	33
trente-quatre	34
trente-cinq	35
trente-six	36
trente-sept	37
trente-huit	38
trente-neuf	39
quarante	40
quarante et un	41
quarante-deux	42
quarante-trois	43
quarante-quatre	44
quarante-cinq	45
quarante-six	46
quarante-sept	47
quarante-huit	48
quarante-neuf	49
cinquante	50
cinquante et un	51
cinquante-deux	52
cinquante-trois	53
cinquante-quatre	54
cinquante-cinq	55
cinquante-six	56
cinquante-sept	57
cinquante-huit	58
cinquante-neuf	59
soixante	60
soixante et un	61
soixante-deux	62
soixante-trois	63
soixante-quatre	64
soixante-cinq	65
soixante-six	66
soixante-sept	67
soixante-huit	68
soixante-neuf	69

quarante-cinq

bons points

- To ask what the time is, you can say either '**il est quelle heure?**' or '**quelle heure est-il?**', which is more formal.

- Do not pronounce the 't' at the end of '**minuit**'.

- Pronounce the 'x' of '**deux**' as if it were a 'z' and run the two words ('**deux**' and '**heures**') together. Do the same with '**six heures**'.

- Pronounce the 's' of '**trois**' as if it were a 'z' and run the two words ('**trois**' and '**heures**') together.

- Pronounce the 'f' of '**neuf**' as if it were a 'v' and run the two words ('**neuf**' and '**heures**') together.

- Do not pronounce the 't' at the end of '**quart**', but don't forget the 'r'.

quarante-six

20 il est quelle heure?

Choose the right caption for each picture and add the time to each clock.

1 a Il est midi. ☐
   b Il est minuit. ☐

2 a Il est une heure et demie. ☐
   b Il est neuf heures moins le quart. ☐

3 a Il est onze heures et quart. ☐
   b Il est sept heures moins le quart. ☐

4 a Il est midi et demi. ☐
   b Il est trois heures et quart. ☐

5 a Il est cinq heures. ☐
   b Il est onze heures et demie. ☐

6 a Il est deux heures. ☐
   b Il est six heures et demie. ☐

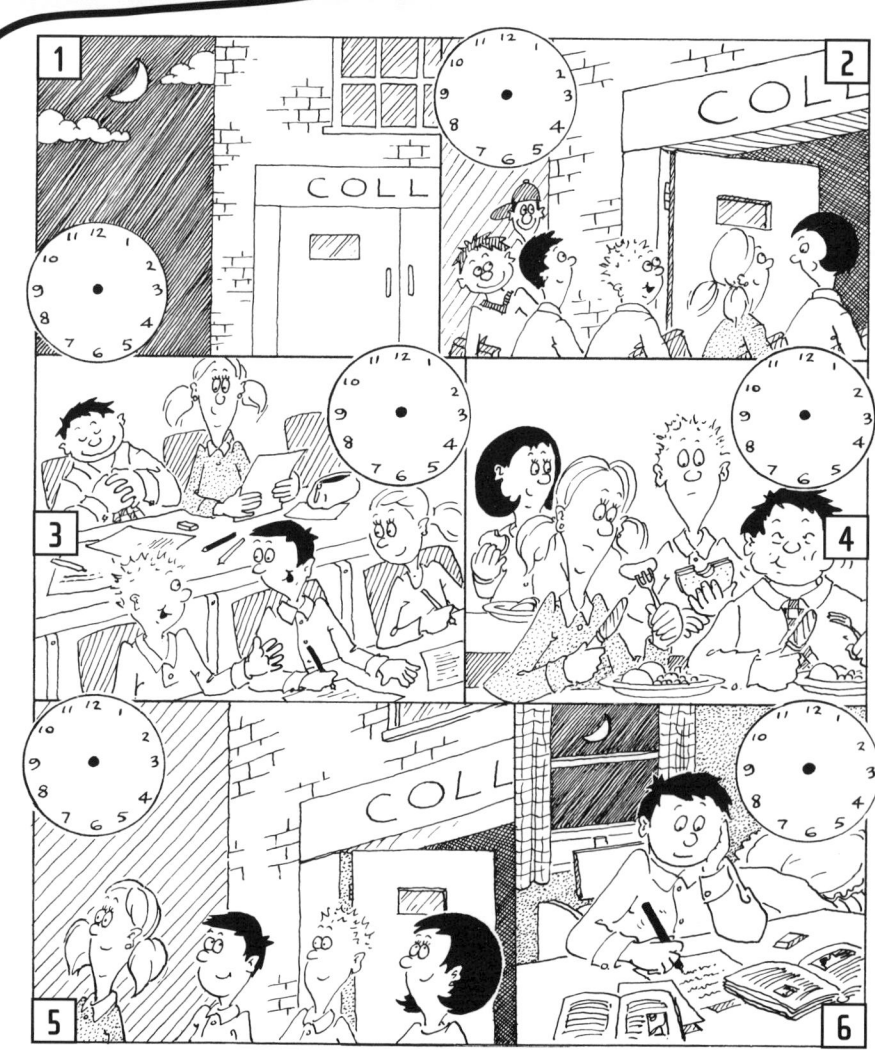

mots croisés

Horizontalement ▶
1 il est 12 heures = il est _____
6 il est 24 heures = il est _____
7 il est trois _____ et demie
10 il est 19 heures = il est ____ heures

Verticalement ▼
2 il est 12 heures 30 = il est midi et _____
3 il est 13 heures 15 = il est une heure et _____
4 il est 20 heures 15 = il est huit heures ___ quart
5 il est 20 heures 45 = il est neuf heures _____ le quart
8 il ___ minuit et demi
9 il est 18 heures = il est ___ heures

mini-dico

l'heure	hour, time, o'clock
il est	it is
quelle heure?	what time?
midi	twelve (midday)
minuit	twelve (midnight)
et demi(e)	half past
et quart	quarter past
moins le quart	quarter to

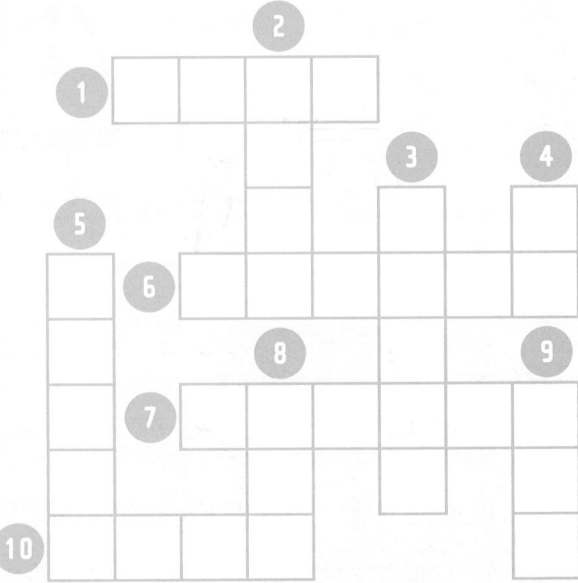

par cœur

Learn this by heart.

Il est midi à Paris,
Neuf heures à Honfleur,
Quatre heures et quart à Colmar,
mais quelle heure est-il à Lille?

quarante-sept

bons points

- Use 'à pied' to say you go on foot.
- Use 'à vélo' to say you cycle.

- Most other means of transport are introduced with 'en' – 'en bus', 'en train', 'en avion'.

21 à pied ou à vélo

Which means of transport are illustrated in this picture?

à vélo ☐
à pied ☐
en bus ☐
en train ☐
en avion ☐
en métro ☐
en voiture ☐
en tramway ☐

moi... moi... moi...

Complete the speech bubble saying how you and your friend go to school, and stick in a picture to illustrate it.

School is BAD

mini-dico

l'avion	aeroplane
le bateau	boat
le bus	bus
le train	train
le tramway	tram
le vélo	bicycle
la voiture	car
à pied	on foot
en bus	by bus

Je vais à l'école ....
Mon copain/Ma copine .... va à l'école ....
....

par cœur

When you have completed the speech bubble, learn it by heart.

Je vais à l'école ...

quarante-neuf

bons points

- Pronounce '**mon anniversaire**' as if '**anniversaire**' started with an 'n'. It is the same for '**bon anniversaire**'.

- In French, '**anniversaire**' can mean either 'birthday' or 'anniversary'.

- Say '**quand**' as if it began with 'k' – do not pronounce the 'u', or the 'd' at the end.

22 bon anniversaire

Find in the grid the French for:

January	....	July	....
February	....	August	....
March	....	September	....
April	....	October	....
May	....	November	....
June	....	December	....

	D	É	C	E	M	B	R	E	S
●	J	A	N	V	I	E	R	N	E
F	É	V	R	I	E	R	J	O	P
A	A	M	J	B	O	M	U	V	T
V	O	N	A	U	A	A	I	E	E
R	Û	N	N	R	I	I	L	M	M
I	T	I	V	E	S	N	L	B	B
L	R	S	A	I	R	E	E	R	R
O	C	T	O	B	R	E	T	E	E

The remaining letters make up a message. What is it?
....

cinquante

moi... moi... moi...

Complete the speech bubbles with details of your birthday and that of your relatives or friends.
Add an illustration.

> C'est quand, ton anniversaire?

> Mon ...., c'est le ....

> C'est quand, l'anniversaire de ta maman/sœur/copine?

> L'anniversaire de ma ...., c'est le ....

> C'est quand, l'anniversaire de ton papa/copain/frère?

> L'anniversaire de mon ...., c'est le ....

mini-dico

l'année	year
l'anniversaire	birthday
janvier	January
février	February
mars	March
avril	April
mai	May
juin	June
juillet	July
août	August
septembre	September
octobre	October
novembre	November
décembre	December
bon anniversaire	happy birthday
quand?	when?

par cœur

When you have completed the bubbles, learn them by heart.

cinquante et un

bons points

- To ask what the weather is like, you can say either **'il fait quel temps?'** or **'quel temps fait-il?'**, which is more formal.

- **'Il fait'** means literally 'it does'. It is used to introduce many weather expressions, such as **'il fait froid'** (it is cold) and **'il fait chaud'** (it is warm).

- Do not pronounce the 'd' at the end of **'froid'** and **'chaud'**. It is the same for **'brouillard'**.

- **'Il pleut'** can mean either 'it rains' or 'it is raining' and **'il neige'** can mean either 'it snows' or 'it is snowing'.

- Do not pronounce the 't' at the end of **'pleut'**. It is the same for **'vent'**.

cinquante-deux

52

23 il fait quel temps?

Are you an optimist? Try this quiz and find out...

En automne, il y a du vent...
▪ ... et du brouillard. Je déteste l'automne.
● J'adore le vent. C'est marrant!

En hiver, il fait froid...
▪ ... très froid. Je déteste l'hiver.
● ... et il neige! J'adore la neige. Super!

Au printemps, il fait moins froid...
● ... et il y a du soleil et des fleurs. C'est génial!
▪ ... et il pleut. Je déteste la pluie.

En été, il y a du soleil. Il fait beau temps...
● ... et il fait chaud. C'est les vacances. J'adore l'été.
▪ ... et il fait chaud... trop chaud. Je déteste l'été.

Tu as 3 ou 4 ● : tu es optimiste. Super!
Tu as 2 ● : tu es dans la moyenne*...
Tu as 3 ou 4 ▪ : tu es pessimiste! Oh, là, là...

*dans la moyenne = average

mots croisés

Horizontalement ▶
4 il neige: il fait _____
5 il ____ beau temps
6 au printemps, il _____
7 en automne, il y a du _____
10 en ___, il fait chaud
11 en hiver, il _____
12 Il fait quel _____ ?

Verticalement ▼
1 en été, il fait _____
2 il y a du _____ : il fait chaud
3 en _____, il fait froid
6 au _____, il fait moins froid
8 en _____, il y a du brouillard
9 en automne, il y a du brouillard et du ____

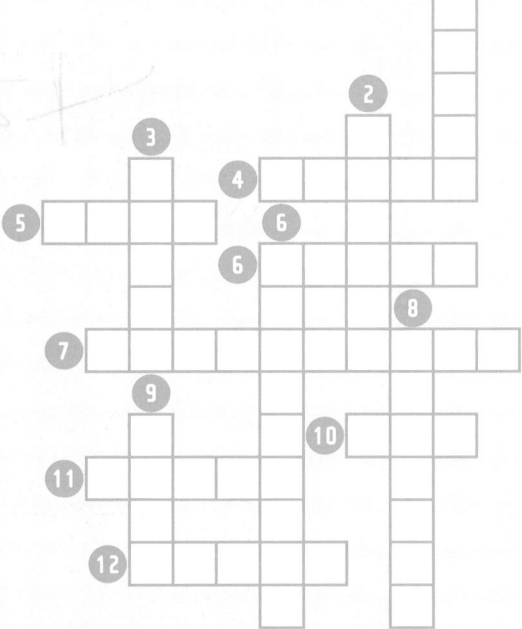

mini-dico

l'automne	autumn
le brouillard	fog
l'été	summer
la fleur	flower
l'hiver	winter
le printemps	spring
le soleil	sun
le temps	weather
le vent	wind
beau	fine
chaud	hot, warm
froid	cold
moins	less
très	very
trop	too
en/au	in
il fait...	it is...
il neige	it snows/ is snowing
il pleut	it rains/ is raining
quel?	what?

par cœur

Learn this by heart.

Au printemps,
Gaétan
Aime les gants blancs.
Mais en hiver,
Il préfère
Les pull-overs
Verts!

cinquante-trois

l'année

bons points

- The French for 70 is literally 'sixty-ten', 71 is 'sixty-eleven', and so on.

- The French for 80 is literally 'four-twenties', 81 is 'four-twenty-one', and so on.

- The French for 90 is literally 'four-twenty-ten', 91 is 'four-twenty-eleven', and so on.

cinquante-quatre

24 récréation

Put the pairs back together.

90	quatre-vingt-un
76	quatre-vingt-dix-huit
80	soixante et onze
72	quatre-vingt-sept
95	soixante-treize
73	quatre-vingt-quatorze
97	soixante-quatorze
88	soixante-seize
74	quatre-vingt-dix
94	soixante-dix
75	quatre-vingt-seize
93	soixante-dix-sept
89	quatre-vingt-onze
77	quatre-vingt-douze
87	soixante-dix-huit
96	soixante-dix-neuf
71	quatre-vingts
84	soixante-quinze
99	quatre-vingt-neuf
78	quatre-vingt-quinze
91	quatre-vingt-six
79	quatre-vingt-deux
81	quatre-vingt-trois
70	cent
82	quatre-vingt-quatre
92	quatre-vingt-cinq
83	quatre-vingt-huit
85	quatre-vingt-treize
100	quatre-vingt-dix-sept
86	quatre-vingt-dix-neuf
98	soixante-douze

pour chanter

This song is popular with French children at Christmas time.
It is sung to the tune of 'Jingle Bells'.

Vive le vent, vive le vent
Vive le vent d'hiver
Qui s'en va sifflant, soufflant
Dans les grands sapins verts.
Vive le temps, vive le temps
Vive le temps d'hiver
Boules de neige et jour de l'an
Et bonne année grand-mère.

mini-dico

soixante-dix	70
soixante et onze	71
soixante-douze	72
soixante-treize	73
soixante-quatorze	74
soixante-quinze	75
soixante-seize	76
soixante-dix-sept	77
soixante-dix-huit	78
soixante-dix-neuf	79
quatre-vingts	80
quatre-vingt-un	81
quatre-vingt-deux	82
quatre-vingt-trois	83
quatre-vingt-quatre	84
quatre-vingt-cinq	85
quatre-vingt-six	86
quatre-vingt-sept	87
quatre-vingt-huit	88
quatre-vingt-neuf	89
quatre-vingt-dix	90
quatre-vingt-onze	91
quatre-vingt-douze	92
quatre-vingt-treize	93
quatre-vingt-quatorze	94
quatre-vingt-quinze	95
quatre-vingt-seize	96
quatre-vingt-dix-sept	97
quatre-vingt-dix-huit	98
quatre-vingt-dix-neuf	99
cent	100
vive	hurrah for
qui s'en va	that goes
sifflant	whistling
soufflant	blowing
le sapin	pine tree
la boule de neige	snowball
le jour de l'an	New Year's Day
bonne année	Happy New Year

cinquante-cinq

 l'année

bons points

- All the boxes in colour represent days that are public holidays in France – there are 11 altogether.

- For the first of a month, write '**1ᵉʳ**', which is short for '**premier**'.

- In France public holidays do not necessarily fall on a Monday.

- Good Friday is not a holiday in France.

- Boxing Day is not a holiday in France.

25 les jours de fête

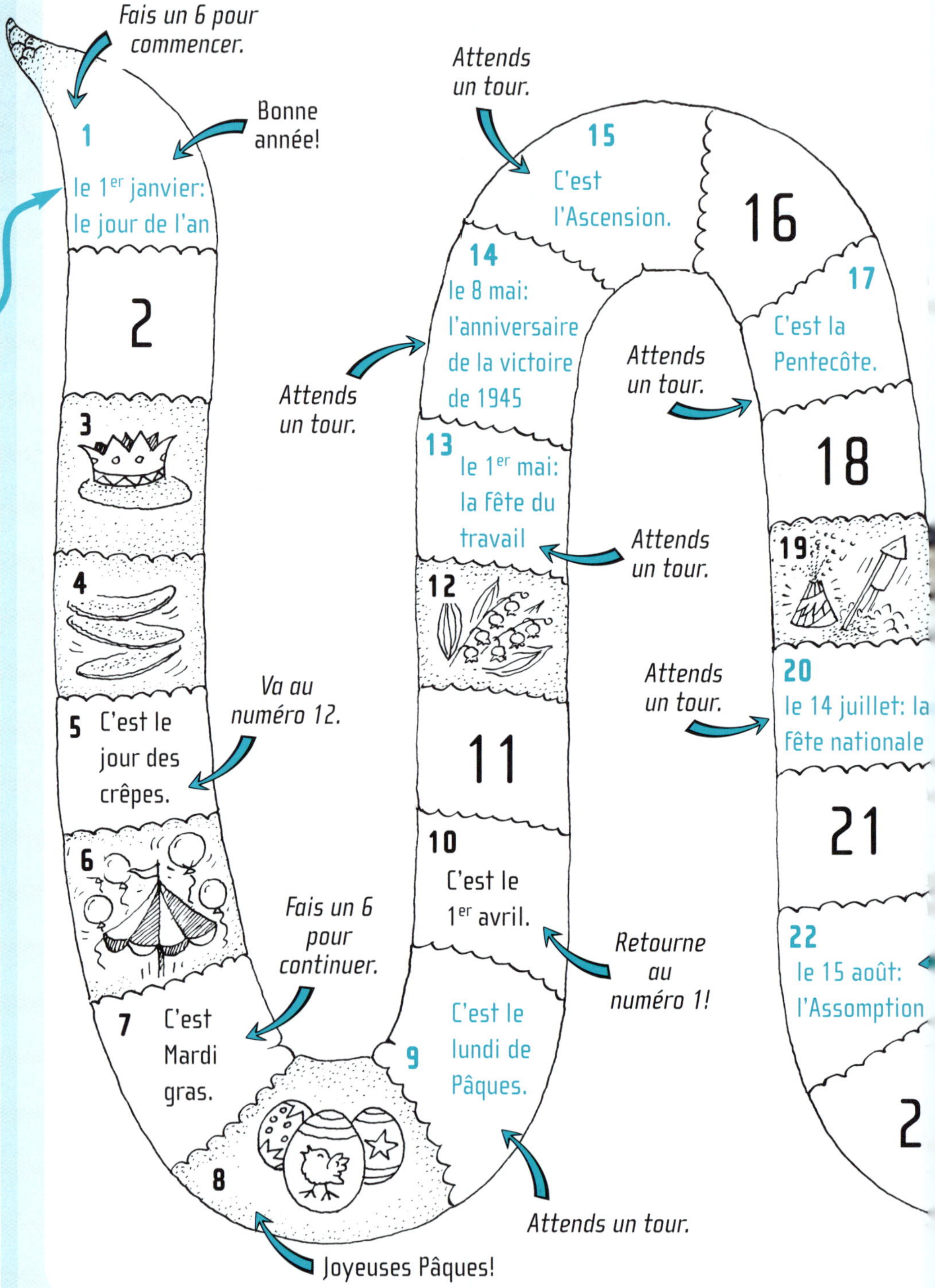

Fais un 6 pour commencer.

1 le 1ᵉʳ janvier: le jour de l'an — Bonne année!

2

3

4

5 C'est le jour des crêpes.

6

7 C'est Mardi gras. — Fais un 6 pour continuer.

8 — Joyeuses Pâques!

9 C'est le lundi de Pâques.

10 C'est le 1ᵉʳ avril. — Retourne au numéro 1!

11

12 — Va au numéro 12.

13 le 1ᵉʳ mai: la fête du travail — Attends un tour.

14 le 8 mai: l'anniversaire de la victoire de 1945 — Attends un tour.

15 C'est l'Ascension. — Attends un tour.

16

17 C'est la Pentecôte. — Attends un tour.

18

19

20 le 14 juillet: la fête nationale

21

22 le 15 août: l'Assomption

Attends un tour.

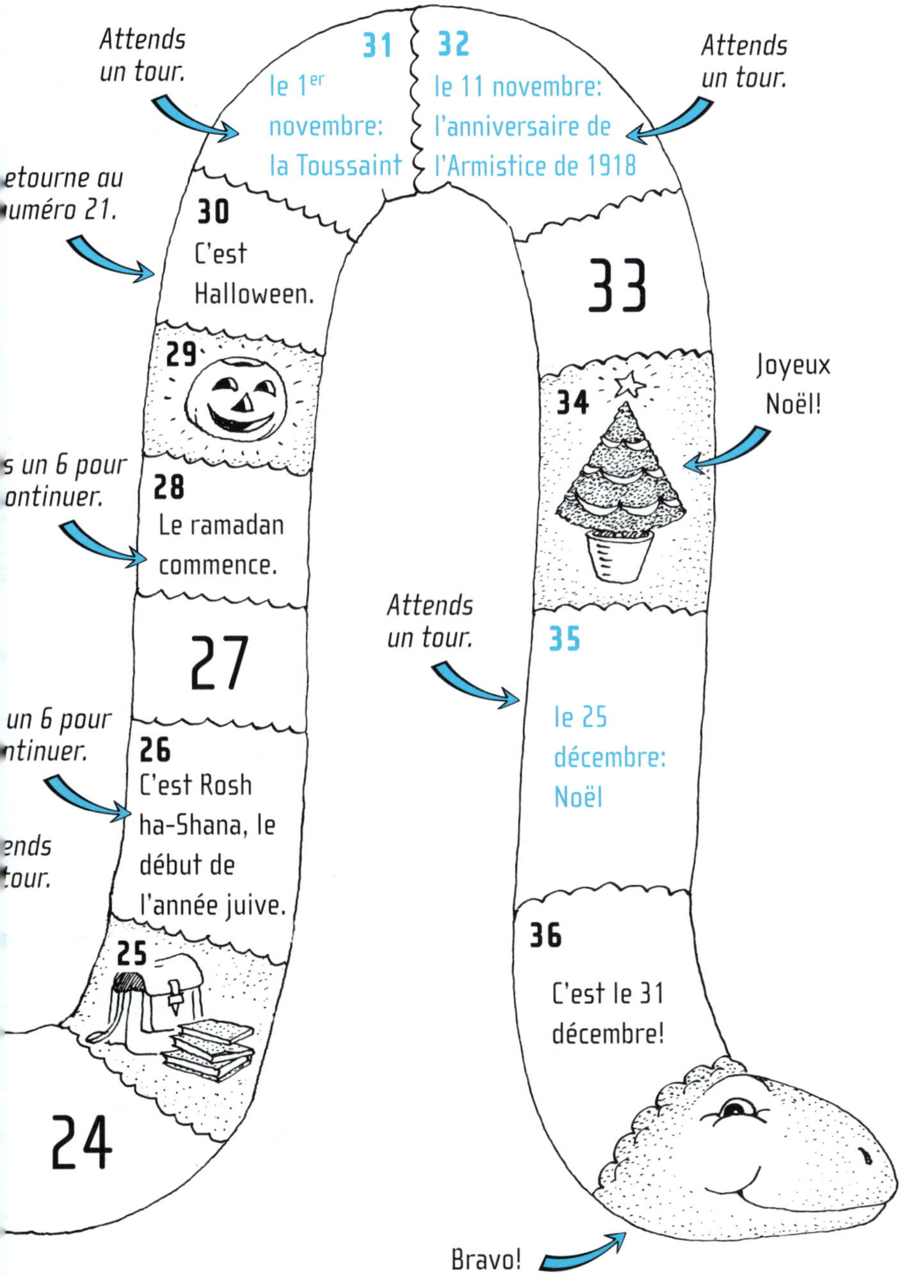

mini-dico

la crêpe	pancake
le début	beginning
la fête	holiday, festival
le jour	day
le Mardi gras	Shrove Tuesday
Noël	Christmas
Pâques	Easter
la Pentecôte	Whitsun
le travail	work, labour
la victoire	victory
juif/juive	Jewish
bonne année	Happy New Year
joyeuses Pâques	Happy Easter
joyeux Noël	Merry Christmas
attends un tour	miss a turn
fais un 6	throw a 6
pour commencer	to start
pour continuer	to continue
retourne	go back

Attends un tour.

31 le 1er novembre: la Toussaint

32 le 11 novembre: l'anniversaire de l'Armistice de 1918

Attends un tour.

Retourne au numéro 21.

30 C'est Halloween.

29

33

28 Le ramadan commence.

Fais un 6 pour continuer.

34 Joyeux Noël!

27

Attends un tour.

26 C'est Rosh ha-Shana, le début de l'année juive.

Fais un 6 pour continuer.

35 le 25 décembre: Noël

Attends un tour.

25

36 C'est le 31 décembre!

24

Bravo!

cinquante-sept 57

réponses

présentations

1 salut (pages 8–9)

- 1 salut, 2 oui, 3 non, 4 au secours, 5 merci, 6 ça va?, 7 ça va, 8 et toi?
- 1 salut!, 2 merci, 3 au secours!, 4 ça va?

2 au revoir! (pages 10–11)

- 1 au revoir, 2 bonsoir, 3 bonjour, 4 bonne nuit, 5 s'il te plaît

3 les numéros (pages 12–13)

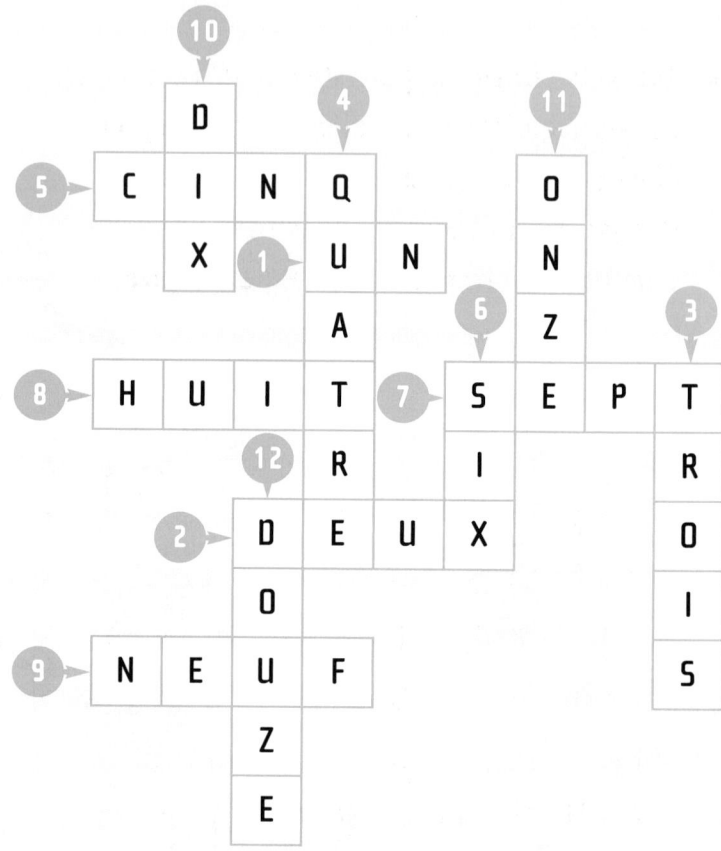

- 2 – Matthieu, 3 – François, six – Alice, 7- Annette, 9 – Monsieur Lebœuf, 12 – Madame Ventouse
- Milou is playing the guitar.

4 tu t'appelles comment? (pages 14–15)

- 1 Tu as quel âge?, 2 Tu t'appelles comment?, 3 Je m'appelle…
- Alex is the youngest (10); Sam is the oldest (12).

cinquante-huit

chez moi

5 tu habites où? (pages 16–17)

- Aberystwyth est au pays de Galles, Birmingham est en Angleterre, Bruxelles est en Belgique, Glasgow est en Ecosse, Chicago est aux USA, Québec est au Canada, Genève est en Suisse, Dublin est en Irlande, Paris est en France

6 ma maison (pages 18–19)

- 1 vrai, 2 vrai, 3 faux, 4 faux, 5 faux, 6 faux
- 1 chambre, 2 jardin, 3 maison, 4 cuisine, 5 salon, 6 escalier, 7 toilettes

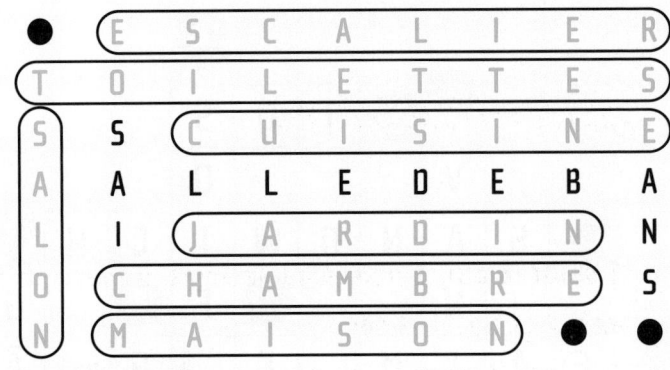

- salle de bains

7 ma famille (pages 20–21)

- 1 frère, 2 sœur, 3 père, 4 mère, 5 grand-père, 6 grand-mère, 7 beau-père, 8 belle-mère, 9 demi-sœur
- B

8 mes animaux (pages 22–23)

- 1 oui, 2 non, 3 oui, 4 non, 5 oui, 6 oui, 7 oui, 8 oui, 9 non, 10 oui

j'aime

9 bon appétit! (pages 24–25)

- A sandwich au poulet, B sandwich au jambon, C pizza aux champignons, D eau minérale, E sandwich au fromage, F limonade, G glace à la fraise, H salade, I glace à la vanille, J gâteau au chocolat, K frites, L jus d'orange

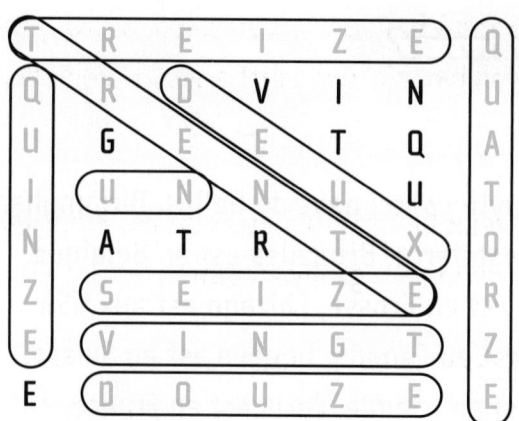

- vingt-quatre
- 1 vingt-cinq, 2 vingt-deux, 3 trente, 4 treize, 5 vingt, 6 dix-neuf

13 mes passe-temps (pages 32–33)

- 1 jouer aux cartes, 2 les ordinateurs, 3 lire, 4 danser, 5 j'aime ça, 6 je déteste ça

le look

10 mes copains (pages 26–27)

- A Hamid, B Julie, C Matthieu, D Karima, E Océane, F Luc

11 le sport (pages 28–29)

- 1 J'aime l'équitation, 2 J'aime la planche à voile, 3 J'aime le basket, 4 J'aime le vélo

12 récréation (pages 30–31)

- There are 9 numbers: treize, un, seize, vingt, douze, quinze, quatorze, deux, trente

14 mes couleurs préférées (pages 34–35)

- les couleurs primaires: red, yellow, blue
  les couleurs complémentaires: red and green, yellow and purple, blue and orange

15 le corps (pages 36–37)

- 1 les yeux, 2 les pieds, 3 les cheveux, 4 les bras, 5 le nez, 6 la tête, 7 le corps, 8 la bouche

16 mes vêtements préférés (pages 38–39)

- 1 le pantalon, 2 la veste, 3 les chaussures, 4 la cravate

soixante

- He is wearing a blue coat, grey jeans, brown (high) boots, a red hat, a green scarf and black gloves.

17 petit ou grand? (pages 40–41)

- 1 les cheveux longs, 2 les yeux bleus, 3 les yeux marron, 4 mince, 5 grand, 6 petit

l'école

18 mes matières préférées (pages 42–43)

- L<u>UNDI</u>, M<u>ARDI</u>, M<u>ERCREDI</u>, J<u>EUDI</u>, V<u>ENDREDI</u>, S<u>AMEDI</u>, D<u>IMANCHE</u>
- sport: b, maths: c, anglais: f, français: g, histoire: h, sciences: e, musique: d, géographie: i, informatique: a
- Samia's timetable

19 récréation (pages 44–45)

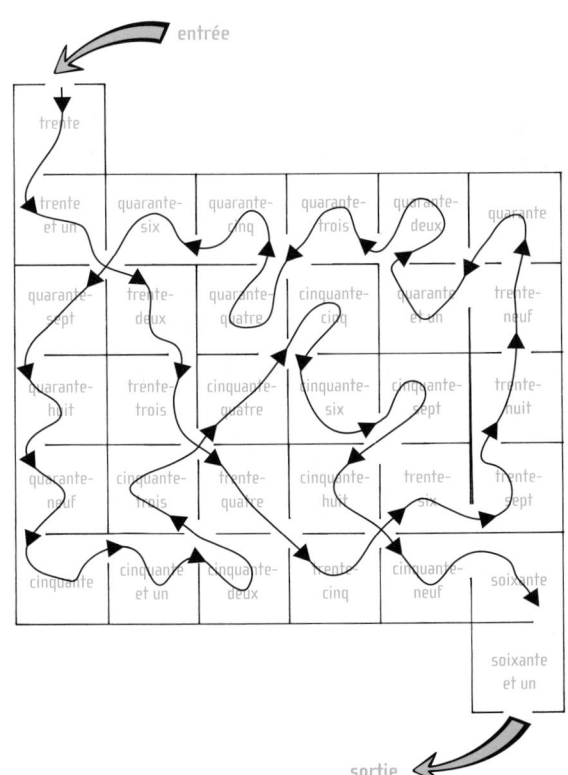

20 il est quelle heure? (pages 46–47)

- 1b, 2b, 3a, 4a, 5a, 6b.

soixante et un

21 à pied ou à vélo (pages 48–49)

- à vélo, à pied, en bus, en train, en avion, en bateau, en voiture

22 bon anniversaire (pages 50–51)

- janvier, février, mars, avril, mai, juin, juillet, août, septembre, octobre, novembre, décembre

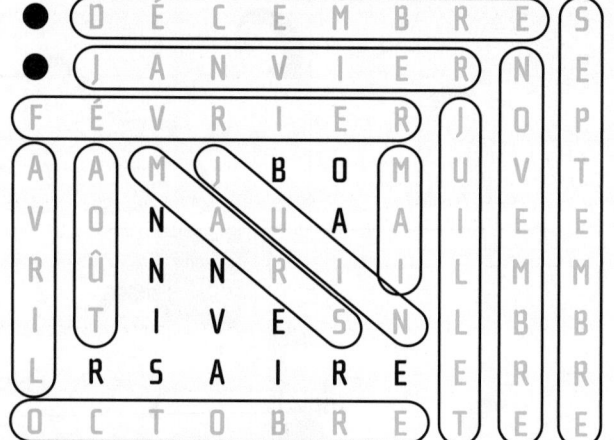

- bon anniversaire

23 il fait quel temps? (pages 52–53)

24 récréation (pages 54–55)

90	quatre-vingt-dix
76	soixante-seize
80	quatre-vingts
72	soixante-douze
95	quatre-vingt-quinze
73	soixante-treize
97	quatre-vingt-dix-sept
88	quatre-vingt-huit
74	soixante-quatorze
94	quatre-vingt-quatorze
75	soixante-quinze
93	quatre-vingt-treize
89	quatre-vingt-neuf
77	soixante-dix-sept
87	quatre-vingt-sept
96	quatre-vingt-seize
71	soixante et onze
84	quatre-vingt-quatre
99	quatre-vingt-dix-neuf
78	soixante-dix-huit
91	quatre-vingt-onze
79	soixante-dix-neuf
81	quatre-vingt-un
70	soixante-dix
82	quatre-vingt-deux
92	quatre-vingt-douze
83	quatre-vingt-trois
85	quatre-vingt-cinq
100	cent
86	quatre-vingt-six
98	quatre-vingt-dix-huit

soixante-deux

Notes

Mon emploi du temps

Heure	lundi	mardi	mercredi	jeudi	vendredi
RÉCRÉATION					
DÉJEUNER					
RÉCRÉATION					

Notes